The Pornstar and the Priest

Words by Ray Hollingsworth
Design by Lee Thomas

©Kiss Production Limited 2001

All photography by Lee Thomas

Except for the poems;
Lost, Space Invaders,
White Dogs on Heat, Steak Pie.
Sourced by Rueben Turner
www.reubenturner.com

Cover design by Jackie Moon

GW00705954

ISBN 0953 6958 16
Printed by Jenner (City Print) Ltd.

Dedicated to Ellen MacArthur

Published by Kiss Production

CONTENTS

This is the bit I didn't write the last time around. It was quite deliberate not to have anything about me at the beginning of my first book, 'The Erotic Café.'

The only ambition I ever have with my work is that people will read it, and hopefully take something from it.

I've actually tried quite hard over the last few years not to read anything of anyone elses. This contravenes the opinion of those in the business who will say otherwise.

If anyone reading this has the ambition to get a book of poetry published, I can tell them now that it's just about impossible. I initially went down the normal route of sending my work to poetry publishers in the UK. I soon realised that the only way to do it was to set up my own publishing company and do everything myself.

I'm glad I did it, it's far more rewarding that way but it's still tough. I was also in the fortunate position of being able to self-finance the initial projects and those that have followed. It has proved to be the most satisfying thing I've ever done - far more so than the businesses I've owned and any employment I was ever in.

I always believed in my work and there have been times when I was totally driven by it. I think it is fundamental that you must believe in your own work for anyone else to believe in it. And if you do, then you should push it out to people. Be relentless and never give up. Otherwise you will never know.

I'm actually writing this on Christmas Day. It is ten past five and I've just taken a pause for a few minutes to watch 'The Bluetones' video of 'If' on MTV2. So although this may not be all that well written, at least you're getting it live and it won't be changed. And you may wonder why anyone would be writing something like this on Christmas Day.

Well, I'm alone (apart from the cat who is sleeping just a few feet away). It is peaceful and tranquil. Incense and candles burn. Sometimes it's good to be alone, to have time and space to think. If you can't find yourself - no one else will find you, but by then you may not wish to be found.

And now it's 'Ocean Colour Scene' at V2000, recorded in August at Chelmsford. And I'm pleased to say I was there both days, and even more pleased that 2 of my daughters were there too.

Excellent music continues to come out of my digital Toshiba television so I'm gonna hit you with some more...'Wide Open Space' by Mansun and 'These Wooden Ideas' by Idlewild, now it's the Stereophonics. I see a lot of live music - perhaps as much as I ever did (but it was much reduced when we were bringing up children).

Thank you, Mark Morriss of The Bluetones for mentioning 'The Erotic Café at Colchester Arts Centre at the warm up gig for Reading. Also thank you to Darren Hayman of Hefner for coming to the Arts Centre twice recently and performing 'Painting and Kissing' which I love so much along with everything that Hefner do so brilliantly. And while I'm thanking people, it was a lovely surprise to hear from Sally Dexter from the cast of 'The Lion, The Witch and The Wardrobe' at Sadlers Wells. I'm glad you liked the book.

Anyway, I'm still coming to you live and I'm just off to put the kettle on and mash some tea (as they used to say in Nottingham, according to Alan Sillitoe). And now it's Moloko - 'Pure Pleasure Seeker' with a video chosen by Soulwax.

One downside that I experienced this morning was the failure of half of the Christmas lights to come on. Temperamental fuckers they are. But the small ones are still working - which is just as well as I only brought them a couple of days ago (they were only £4.95).

Visitors to my house will remember that a year ago I thought the Christmas lights and my silver tree looked so lovely that I kept them up until Easter.

So you've shared a few moments of Christmas Day with me, whoever you are and wherever you are. Follow your hopes and follow your dreams. Follow your intuition. Be brave. Be eternally grateful for the life that God gave you.

Finally, I was on a crowded tube train this year which was stuck somewhere between Kings Cross and Farringdon (that won't surprise anyone who travels on the circle line), and feeling pretty crap when I noticed a little girl, about 5, with her mother and the child gave her mother the most beautiful smile.

From that moment everything came into perspective. Things like this stay with you forever. We are surrounded by beauty but some of us can never see it. Next time you hear the birds sing, listen closer. We live on an amazing planet. Live the dream.

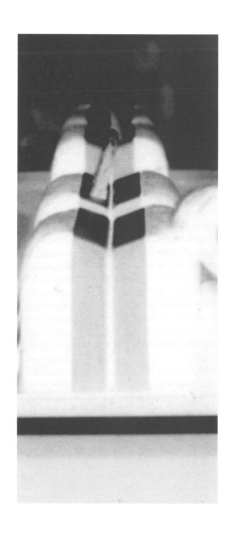

SILENT WITNESS

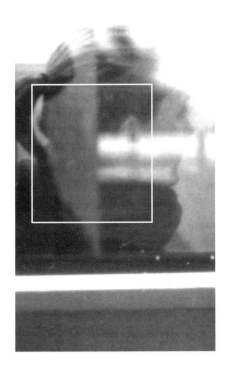

and maybe if I saw you

on a crowded railway station

in the liquid crystal evening

would I stop to take a photo

in case you never happened

I could have been mistaken

but somehow I don't think so

then imagine if I caught

your reflection in a window

sometime in the future

at a modern retail outlet

where the dreams are half price

and the staff are european

would I summon up the courage

it's a tough one to call

it's not that I don't mean to

I'm sure you've got the picture

HACKNEY MOON

it's
four
o'clock
in
the
high
rise

your
body
rocks
in
the
blue
skies

the
pastel
walls
and
the
duvet

the
magazines
and
the
hairspray

the silence
of
the
tv
chat
show

death
in
vegas
on
the
radio

the
sunlight
that
kisses
you
softly
on
the
shoulder

moments
live
forever
but
one
day
we'll
grow
colder

sleep
softly
so
very
softly
silent
one

your
star
shines
in
the
east
and
the
hackney
moon
has
come

LOST

there
beside us
our picture
looks out
from the past

like an
act in
a play
in which
we were
cast

laying
in our bed
of former
dreams
but now
a place
of silent
screams

under cover
of the dark
the wonder
of the
loving spark

lost in
some
underground
carpark
where
you danced
in bare feet

lost on
some remote
winter morning
on a
shingle beach

you are
here
but you

are out
of reach

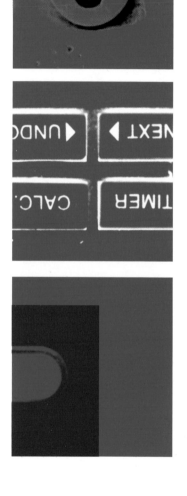

TOUCHTONE

thank you
for calling
the paramedic
emergency
hotline

if you have
a touchtone
telephone
please press 5

thank you

if you would
like to hear
about our home
delivery service
on pork and beef
sausages
please press 1

If you would
like to hear
about super-smooth
nails on our
beauty line
please press 2

if you would
like tips on
making your
salad cream
last longer
please press 3

If you would
like to hear
about our new
loyalty card
scheme
please press 4

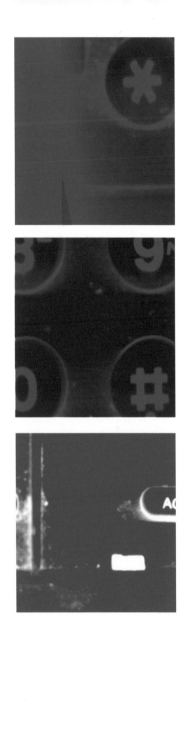

If you are
having a
heart attack
please press 5

thank you

all of
our advisors
are busy
at the moment
if you think you
may be dying
please press 6

thank you

if you think
you may have
less than 5 minutes
to live
please press 7

thank you

if you would
like to hear about
our special offers
on teflon
saucepans
please press 8

steve morris
aged 47
died in a
semi detached
near you

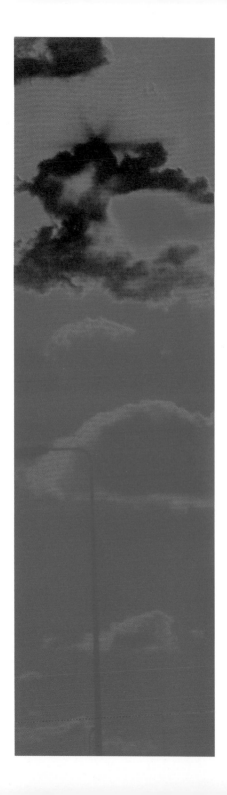

M.o.D

poor little star
fell
from the sky

landed on
a telephone wire

a clergyman
arrived
on an open topped bus
to offer
prayers
and take
photographs

children
from local schools
brought flowers
sang hymns
and circled the area
with
a daisy chain

then
the army came

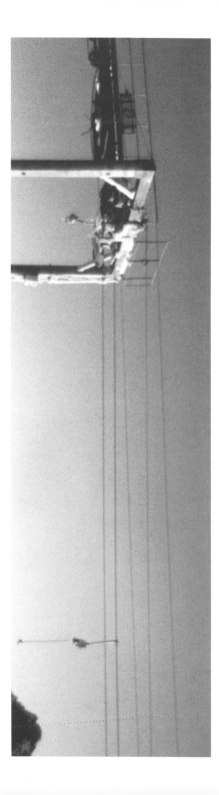

NIKE TRAINERS

mother

have joined the latvian army

we're invading tunisia at dawn

i'm taking a packed lunch

don't wait up

tell chloe not to worry

this is what i want

i've thought about it for 30 seconds

can you phone work

tell them i won't be in

not for a couple of years

if ever

i need a break

from the same old stuff

day in

day out

and the nike trainers

you were getting for my birthday

don't buy them

not just yet

just in case

something goes wrong

which it shouldn't

but you never know

tell dad i won't make saturday's match

or any other

for the rest of the season

but to save the programmes

and the write ups

i can't get the results in the desert

you won't be able to text me

they take away our phones

and destroy them

with all the other junk

that we acquire

and the metal from body piercing

they melt it down

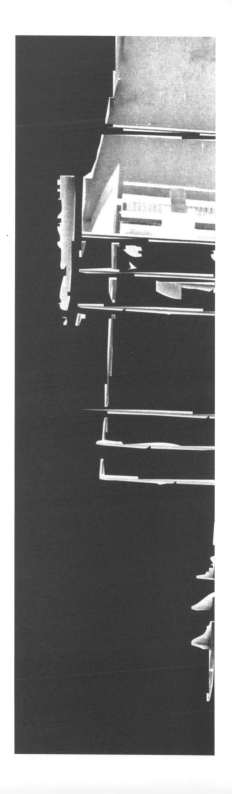

and make direction signs

and what was i thinking of

with the eyebrow ring

it was really naff

i can see that now

but at the time

it seemed really cool

they say they'll cleanse us

from all that shite

that we're immersed in

and i won't have access

to nine hundred channels

which is a relief

'cause i couldn't concentrate

on any one thing

for more than a minute

sometimes seconds

and that dating channel

what a load of crap

all those weird people

looking for love

and do i love chloe?

i'm not really sure

which must tell me something

it was her body

and her hot tongue kissing

but not her soul

i wanted it all

and will i miss the town

i don't think so

i just felt like i was swirling around

in a giant dustbin

and everyone was in it with me

i know this is for the best

i hope you'll understand

your loving son

darren

Top

PAROXIDE

crack babies float on paroxide rivers the naked city shivers in the RAZOR blade morning

pink slabs choke in the pollution and the poison (it's now showing at a cinema near you)

PAROXIDE

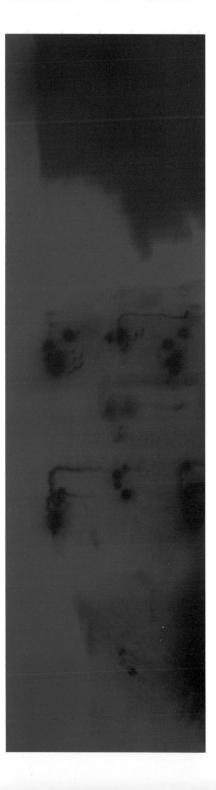

THE CANCER
OF THE CITY

beware

the black eyed

stranger

who emerges

from the

shadows

her make-up

smeared

and fading

in the

twilight

of the summer

her posture

tired and

weary

she beckons

for a light

and invites you back

to her place

in the

moonlit neon night

and from

her attic window

she scans

the city skyline

the tower blocks

and the pylons

the police chase

and the

sirens

and talks

of better days

and of friends

she used to know

and slowly

I am drawn

by her sadness

and her beauty

though she is

tarnished and

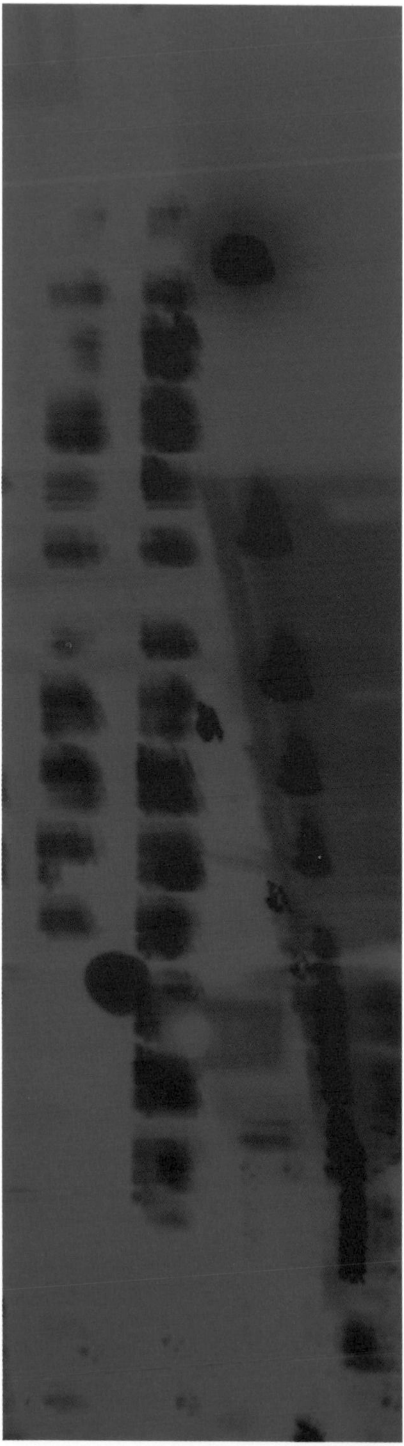

she's tainted
by the cancer
of the
city
and in her
space she
reminisces
blows smoke rings
in the air
with visions
of her mother
and the dress
she used to wear
and the sounds
of her sisters
as they played out
in the rain
in the heartland
of the city
before the missiles
came

GET
ГОК
HE

АРЕ

ESCAPE

...polite conversations
with friends
familiar situations
with him
drifting

evenings of TV
is this her destiny

5p 10p OR 20p COINS

'OU
EN
RF

and on saturday
they go
to tesco
where she
wanders
between the aisles
for miles
drifting
screaming
dreaming
of a new horizon
of the scent of freedom
and relief
from the tedium
of life
as she knows it.

PORNSTAR

she's the
kursal flyer
on the
high tides
the x-rated
pornstar
in the
classifieds
she's a
toxic cocktail
now on
release
a phone call
away from
the catholic
priest
she's the
warning sign
near
chemical waste
a night
on a payphone
at premium
rates

she's 10
different names
on 10
different cards
she's the
danger
that breeds
in every
schoolyard
she's the
face that
you see
in the heat
of the night
she's the
shape on
the screen
as you
turn out
the light

bring on beauty
long live
the beast

STAR

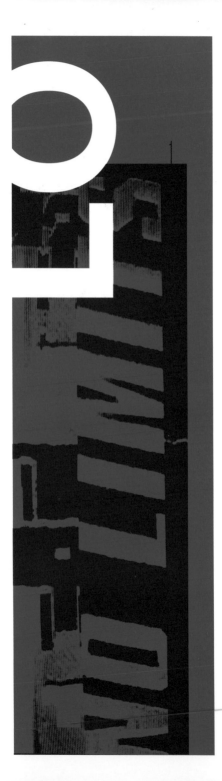

LOVE HEARTS

polyurethane shrink wrap babes of a channel hopping nation   bye products from

sillycone estate the featherlite generation   dermatolically tested to minimise the

risk of intelligent conversation   uniquely shaped to enhance comfort the lubricated

nonoxynol 9 sensation   (available in packs of 5 million)

HE

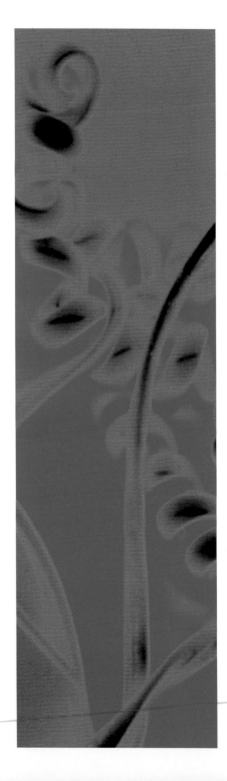

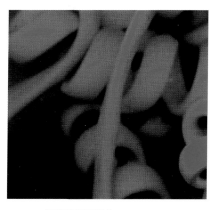

QUICKDIAL

I'll ave

a chicken korma

'an a

popadom

make it

large

make it

dot.com

I'll 'ave

a pepperoni

pizza

with

an

antenna

on

I wan'

it now

make it dot.com

I'll ave

a pint

of lager

and a

digital

coke

'gis a

cd rom

that I

can smoke

I'll have

a quickdial

burger

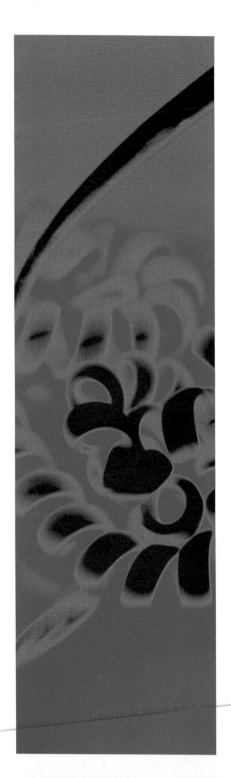

and

modular

fries

stick

some

metal

through

me 'ed

like the

other guys

give me

a price to

double glaze

my floor

100% off

if you

tattoo

the door

buy a

wife

get a

second one

free

get

a life

at the

touch of

a key

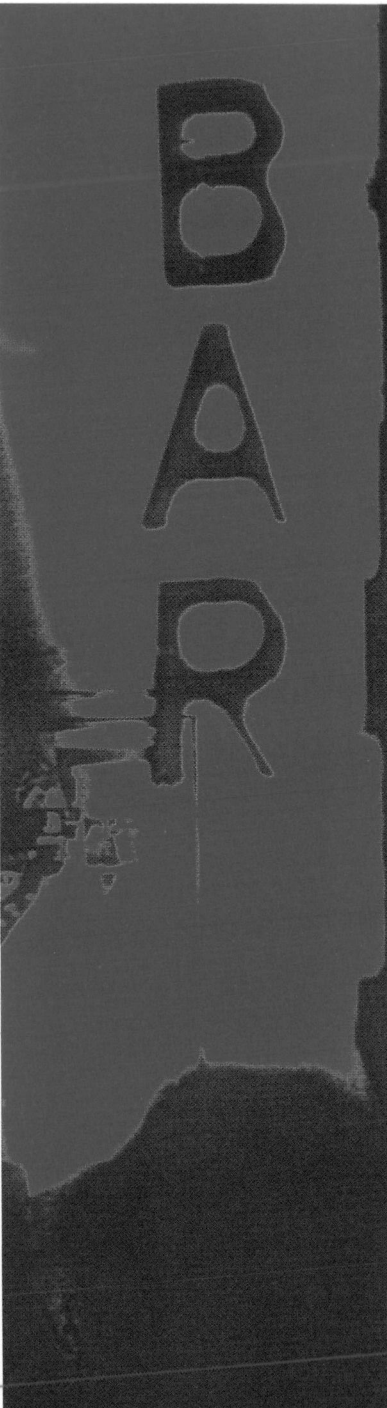
BAR

WHITE DOGS ON HEAT

white dogs

on heat

twilight angels

on the mean streets

sultry shadows

on a loosing streak

insider trading

on the back seat

chemical warfare

and a mercy mission

the childlike prayer

at dawns submission

white dust

and a stolen gun

stiletto ghost

thy kingdom come

Carol woz ere lovin

the suicide note

that no-one found

the milk white skin

on the bloodstained ground

the four year old

that heard her screams

a face in the mirror

in a frozen dream

a polaroid picture

of her dad

the only memory

she ever had

EVERY SHADOW

to think

that I

worshiped the ground

your every word

your every sound

and every

shadow that you cast

and every movement

and each expression

the very fabric

of your being

in this lifetime

all that I believed in

your name

emblazoned

across the skyline

the haunting fragrance

that never dies

each atom

and every sinew

every breath

upon your pillow

forever dance

forever dream

when time

stood still

I caught the moment

you are gone

you are here

you are lost

you are near

in this lifetime

all that

I believed in

SHARON AND KAYLIEGH
BASILDON 1991

my doorta

christ wha's she like

thirt een an finks

she knows it all

ates school

pop stars all over er wall

goes ta raves finks Im er slave

nics all me fags

says that I nag

called me a bag

the little cow

I blame it on er dad

e use to drive me mad

with eeze boozin

christ I was glad

when e fucked off

with that tart from Canvey...

...funny really

we were really appy

when we first met

used ta call me

is little pet

we was always oldin ans

and makin plans

e used ta come ta bingo

seemed ta know all the lingo

but that was 10 years ago

don't seem possible

still we ad some good years
before all the tears
and the fightin

fridays we used ta get
a takeaway
he'd always pay
your treat hed say
and a bottal of wine
things were fine
then
and christmas
ed get me anyfing
cloves
an this diamon ring
I'll always keep it

an when we ad
kayliegh
she was a beautiful baby
we ad it all
nice home car
everyfing

then e startid gettin in
late from work
an there was the
lipstick on is shirt
e always denied there
was anyfing goin on
but I wernt stupid
said it was is mates
messin about
avin a laugh e said
an us only just wed

then he started drinkin
more and more
got stopped by the law
served im right
it did
bloodi fridge was full
of larga
e was always
down the supamarket
buying the stuff
couldn't get enuff
must a bin
costin a fortune

then e started avin
time off work
e couldn't bloode get up
in the mornin
e got a warnin
I wernt surprised
he shoulda realised
jobs are ard to come by

an the mortgage
it got in arrears
it musta bin
goin on beer the monee like
or sumfin
perhaps it was
goin on er

e told me ta get a job

earn a few bob

e said

so I did

earned a hundred quid

a week

selling double glazin

but I knew it was too late

we were gettin in a state

with all the bills

an I was takin pills

for me nerves...

...it was a relief

really when e went

but Kayliegh well

she took it bad

said she missed er dad

I'll never forgive im for that

I fink it really affected er

perhaps thats why shes

like it taday

but shes my doorta

an I'll always love er

I really ope she

meets someone nice

one day

but fings ave

changed

nuffin seems to

last anymore.

1

INVADERS

ROBERT PARKER
PLEASE COME HOME
OR RING ME
THERE ARE NO PROBLEMS
LOVE MUI XXXXXXX

SPACE INVADERS

they've become
regular visitors
on sunday mornings
around eleven
i'm usually in
the dining room
with the times
and gold blend made with
condensed milk
anyway nadia
who is incredibly polite
has taken to
inviting them in
they used to be
quite content
standing on
the doorstep
then being the
perfect hostess
nadia offers them
chocolate biscuits
she has always excelled
in making everyone
feel welcome
even the idiot
window cleaner
who fell through
the conservatory roof
she put a bandage
on his head
and gave him
an aspirin
she befriended
the paper boy
the one who
got caught
selling ecstasy
on the estate
twelve i think
he was
sometimes i think
she can be too friendly
which is why
i was concerned
this weekend
to find her
reciting a passage
from genesis
to an audience
of three
and the cat
all this
and just two days
before her
fifth birthday

GATWICK 3AM

no red carpet
no heroes welcome
no champagne

no fanfare
no hands
to greet us
no shelter
from the rain

no friendly faces
no airs and graces
no satellite crew

no dignatories
no celebrities
no one from
the news

no microphones
no cables
no tables
can't see no
flashing lights

it's just

another
lonely night

but tonight
the stars shine
just for us
and the
cool breeze blows
and whispers
freedom

and the moon
looks down
and smiles
then dances
'cross the sky
as the oceans roar
their approval

and as the sun
lights up
the night
I feel
your little hand
in mine
and I know
that I
was only
dreaming

THIS SALE

IF THE TERMINATION IS AT ZERO
BEFORE DELIVERY COMMENCES

MINIMUM DELIVERY 2 LINES

FUEL CRISIS

You need
commitment
I need excitement
you crave
the comfort
of a peace
agreement
someone reliable
I cannot be
relied upon
to satisfy
your tactile nature
especially
on fridays
I get distracted
by some great divide
a turning tide
restless like
the waves
I never gave
my word
so I
can never break it
and if I leave
my heart
in a rear view mirror
sadly
it will not be yours

THIS SALE

MINIMUM DELIVERY 2 LITRES

LITRES

PENCE PER LITRE

so please
don't ask me
to explain
what I'm torn
between
when I was born
to dream
of new horizons
I didn't
write the script
not that I'm aware
it goes much deeper
you may
find the answer
on some psychology channel
while you're
scrolling pages
in the heartbreak
hours of autumn
I learned not
to promise
what I could not
deliver
and by the time
she arrives
I may be
running
on empty

STEAK PIE

tender chunks
of flesh
topped with a light tan

remove her outer
packaging
dress her in foil
place in a pre-heated
Dulux painted bedroom
for 40 minutes
(adjust times according to room
temperatures -fan assisted rooms
cooking time should be less)

check she
is piping hot
before consuming

we are happy to refund or replace any product
who falls below the high standard you expect.
You may however detect the occasional love bite
on the goods.

If so ask a member of staff for assistance.
This does not affect your statutory rights.

7AM
a small
black
hairbrush
with the
handle
missing
lonely
in the
kitchen
in the
stillness
and the
silence
the CD's
on the
carpet
her
lipstick

on the
wineglass
the
early
morning
shadows
the
reflections
and the
echoes
sacred
like the
sunrise

COLCHESTER 2AM

taxi drivers
will trade secrets
and deliver
crash test
dummies
to remote
farm houses
at 2am
(and stargaze
for 45 minutes)

a surprisingly
high proportion
of silicone
implanted women
(who live on
my estate)
will fake
orgasms

security cameras
will capture
at least
5 lesbian
acts in
multi-story
car parks
by the same
2 fourteen
year old
schoolgirls
(who don't
go to school)

a wino
(born glasgow
1949
but looking
much older)
will witness
a ghost dance
in the
graveyard
near the
derelict hospital
and be
found dead
the next
morning
by a
34 year old
man walking
a creature
resembling
a puma

a motorcyclist
delivering a
pepperoni pizza
will be in
collision with
a green
fluorescent milk
float after
being distracted
by a number
of naked people
fucking
in a phonebox

a catholic priest
will put
48 pornographic
videos in
a black
bin liner
and dump
them in
the playground
of an infant
school
then attempt
to hang
himself in a
bus shelter
(one with
a poster for
scottish widows)
before being
distracted by
an army
helicopter crashing
into a
petrol station

screams will
be heard
in the
subway near
lloyds tsb
as a 31
year old
woman police
officer clad in
metal chains
is raped
by a fox
as disinterested
onlookers eat
shiesh kebabs
and piss
against the
wall

We are surrounded by beauty

but some of us can never see it.

Next time you hear the birds sing

Listen closer.

We live on an amazing planet.

Live the dream.